# Perform Your Own Background Checks

# How to Screen Potential Tenants, Babysitters, Dates, Associates and More

BENJAMIN TIDEAS

# CONTENTS

# INTRODUCTION

I want to congratulate you for finding this book, "Perform Your Own Background Checks - How to Screen Potential Tenants, Babysitters, Dates, Associates and More".

This book contains proven steps and strategies on how to secure background information on the people you may potentially allow into your business or personal life. Most of all, it will give you the tools to bring you peace of mind.

Now more than ever, it is important to have the right knowledge to back you up on vital decisions that have anything to do with your family and personal affairs. With the right tools and information in your hands, it would be easier for you to transact with people, assured in the knowledge that you are dealing with the right kind of individuals either on a professional or personal level.

New for the 2nd Edition, I've included a TON of new resources to help you in your quest to obtain the information you are searching for, in addition to online Additional Resources that I hope you will find very helpful.

Thanks again for picking up this book, now let's get to it!

# BETTER SAFE THAN SORRY

What could be scarier than having to deal with strangers, right? Here you are entrusting a part of your finances, the lives of your loved ones, even your own, in the hands of people you have not met before. But no matter how frightening situations like these are, it is rather inevitable that we would have to deal with strangers at one point or another. We cannot be left on our own. We need the help or companionship of others in order for us to get by. So how do you go about this?

The surest way of ensuring your security is by having the right tools and knowledge to give you the upper hand if things do not go as planned. You do this not out of paranoia, but as a way of safeguarding your own life, the lives of people you love, and the things you have worked hard for. It is also a way of keeping your sanity intact; after all, having the most essential information at your disposal easily quashes notions of distrust and hesitation, which are verily the same things that may keep you from sleeping well at night.

This need to screen people you will have personal or business relationship with is rooted in the idea that not all people can be trusted. You can be the world's biggest optimist, but at the end of the day, there will always be people who may take advantage of you. It is therefore necessary to strike a balance between being trustful and cautious, because excess of one or the other will not result in anything good. Being trustful connotes naiveté and a sense of immaturity, an attitude that is not in touch with the realities of the world. On the other hand, being overly cautious shows a complete lack of trust and confidence in the inherent goodness of other people. Not only is this unfair on many levels, it is also utterly unhealthy.

## Warranted Background Check

When is doing a background check on somebody a warranted exercise? If you are a landlord with a few units to rent out, you may want to screen your potential tenants. This is important because you do not want to have a difficult and problematic tenant occupying any of your property. Just like what they usually say in real estate: An empty unit is so much better than one occupied by a loose screw for a tenant.

There are many ways to screen possible tenants. One of the better ways of doing it is by conducting a credit check. Pulling someone's credit history is great at assessing his/her financial history, as well as his/her ability to meet the financial obligations stated in the lease. In checking this information, pay particular attention to late payments, defaults, or even cases of bankruptcy. It would also do well to take some time to check unpaid balances or credit card balances. Having a look at this information will help you determine if the potential tenant is able to carry out payments in the future. If the credit assessment looks a little off, you may want to harbor second thoughts. To conduct a credit check, you'll need the person's full name, any aliases, their current address, and social security number. Have the applicant sign a credit authorization, and have a company online pull a tri-merge to get access to the information you are looking for.

It would be to your advantage if you do a basic assessment of an applicant's public records, including criminal records, if any. In most states, criminal records can be checked through public records made available online by the Department of Correctional Services. A tenant with a problematic history with the law, or someone who had spent time behind bars may not exactly be the person you are looking for. Having an ex-convict for a tenant may give rise to fear among other tenants wary of their own security.

Part of the background check includes doing interviews with the tenant's former landlords or landladies. This will allow you to check this tenant's prior history. Do you have a tenant with a sketchy background? It might be better to hold off on that application and dig deeper.

Take note, however, that tenants are entitled to their own rights. As a landlord or a landlady, you can only do so much to do background checks without running afoul with existing legislation, such as the Landlord and Tenant Act. Make sure that you also set your screening within the parameters of what is acceptable and legal. Keep tabs of the provisions in the Fair Credit Reporting Act. Unfortunately, you can't just use any service if you're performing a background check as a landlord or employer – for credit, medical and insurance reasons. Among others, the law states that a tenant cannot be discriminated against based on his/her race, physical form, skin color, religion, sex, and family status. If you do reject a potential tenant or employee (even a semi-informal employee like a babysitter) because of a non-CRA background check, you could wind up in legal trouble with the Federal Trade Commission!

At the end of it all, never forget to conduct a face to face interview with a possible tenant. Ask questions to ensure that he/she is a good fit to who you think should occupy your property. Check information relevant to the rent, such as having pets, friend or relatives sleeping over, and details about his/her work. Do not go overboard, though. You want to make sure that you sound as professional as possible, and not some creepy person out for unnecessary personal details.

# GOING IN BLIND...AND INFORMED

It used to be fun doing blind dates. The prospect of meeting somebody without some form of expectations from both ends spells a fascinating night ahead. Or even if the whole thing does not turn out the way you want to, the excitement and thrill generated by your anticipation of how it will all pan out is usually enough not to question the wisdom behind blind dates.

But today's era does not call for hopeless optimism anymore, at least not in the age of Google. It would be foolish not to use the resources available right before your fingertips to find out who your date is going to be. But more than getting the basic information about a particular person, it is now also very easy to take a look at this person's character based on his/her footprints on the Web.

When screening potential dates, Google is one of your best friends. Whoever knew that the world's most popular search engine could turn out to be your greatest ally against bad dates, right? These days, getting the low-down on somebody via Google is as easy as finding your way around the city's terrain via GPRS.

### Digging Ethics

First, consider the ethics involved in digging up information about a person you will have a date with. Why is it necessary to know beforehand how a person looks, thinks, or views things before you meet him/her personally? The answer lies in an instinctive desire both to protect yourself from possible harm and have some sort of reassurance that you are not committing a mistake. So how do you do it?

## Getting Busy

For starters, key in the name of your target in the Google search bar enclosed in quotation marks to filter out irrelevant results and add specifics that might help make your results more relevant (i.e. "John Doe" Providence). This will yield a number of results, but you should be able to find those that relate to the person you are doing a background search on, in this case perhaps, a guy named John Doe who lives or has association to the city of Providence. The level of difficulty of weeding out items from the name search varies, depending on the extent of this person's presence on the Web. Take a look at which sites the person's name appears most frequently on. Are these valid and legitimate sites? Based from this, you can immediately make a general assessment of what type of a person your future date is. For instance, does his/her name crop up on news sites? He/she may be a hotshot. Does his/her name appear on blogs of general interest? This person must have a lot of friends. If his/her name appears on mostly sketchy sites, such as, say, adult forums, then that should serve as a possible red flag.

It is possible to go beyond Google to ascertain the character of your date. In this day and age where a huge part of people's lives is available online, it should not at all be too difficult to learn what a person is up to based on what he reads, posts, and likes on his online accounts. This is particularly more pronounced on social networking sites, where tons of data can be found. To learn about rummaging data through these kinds of sites, refer to Chapter 4, "Sifting through Social Networks."

BONUS RESOURCE: In addition to Whitepages.com and 411.com for basic contact information, check out our additional resources guide online for more dirt! www.plaid-enterprises.com/bgc

# TAKE FEEDBACK FROM OTHERS

While it is almost de rigueur for you to go online should you need some information, there are cases where you have to do things the old-school way. That means picking up the phone to talk to real and actual people, or even set up an appointment for a personal interview. Either way, these situations negate taking feedback from others as a way of getting assured that the decision you are about to make is right.

One of such instances is when you need to hire a babysitter. A babysitter saves the day, particularly when you have to go out for an important social or business function. Whether you are a working professional or a stay-home parent, there are errands you need to attend to and things you have to do out of the house. This is particularly difficult if you have to leave your children at home. As such, a babysitter whom you can trust is without a doubt a life-saver.

## Talk to references

The best way to screen a babysitter is by hearing referrals from people he/she has worked with in the past. Take feedback from others. Ask these people how this person is as a babysitter, or if they have encountered any trouble with him/her. Make sure to let them know how this person worked with their children, or if there is anything that you should know before hiring the services of this person.

Ensure that you have a brief chat with a potential babysitter's references. These references should be able to confirm positive traits about the person, as well as provide verbal recommendations if you ever need one. These will serve as positive assurances that your children will be in good hands while you are away.

Getting feedback from others is also important if you are partnering up with someone for a business or financial venture. Money issues can be really complicated, so you want to make sure that the person you chose to deal with regarding money matters is someone you fully trust and know. It would be a little scary if you proceed to ink partnerships with people whose character and personality you are not completely in the know of.

Most of these financial dealings usually involve people you know working as the bridge between you and your business partners. This is an organic part of networking; where you meet people through mutual acquaintances, and from there proceed to do business. But as with most things, it would be best to proceed with caution. One of the ways to show cautiousness is by screening people you will have future business ventures with. You do this as a way of preventing problems in the future and as a way of making you feel more at ease with the transaction, confident in the knowledge that you are dealing with a person you trust and believe in.

Begin by asking mutual acquaintances about what they know regarding a particular person. Be careful not to sound like you are snooping on someone. You are not. What you are doing is trying to establish the credibility of someone you will be working with. As with any venture, trust should be at the core of everything. It would be difficult to proceed with business if you do not have your partner's full confidence, and vice versa.

BONUS RESOURCE: Tips on How to Check Business References (source: ehow.com)

• Standardize reference checks so that you are obtaining the same information about every candidate. Have that set of questions in front of you when you make a call. At the very least you should verify the facts of a prospective employee's previous work including dates of employment and job titles.

• Call job references when both you and the reference have the time and freedom to discuss a candidate. Block out a generous amount of time to talk. It's better to have more than not enough. If you can't reach a reference initially, call her back instead of leaving a detailed message. It will ensure both the candidate's and the references' privacy. If you must leave a message, be as general as possible, giving your name and a number at which to return your call.

• Make note of with whom you are speaking and their association with your candidate. This will vary depending on the company's reference policy. A person who has worked with your candidate in a supervisory position can provide a more in-depth profile than Human Resources personnel.

• Identify yourself, your company and the purpose of your call. Explain a little bit about the vacant position and ask whether he feels the candidate's qualifications fit the job, allowing him to elaborate as he sees fit. Interrupting or redirecting the conversation when a reference is still speaking can limit the amount of substantive information you receive.

• Ask for specifics about the candidate's work responsibilities and how he fulfilled those responsibilities. Clarify any vague statements, making sure to summarize what it is you think has been said. Using a summary statement may make it easier for a reference to overcome any hesitation she has in responding fully to further questions.

• Thank the contact for his time and ask if you may contact him again if you have further questions.

• Ensure a candidate has given express permission to contact references prior to making any calls, and check only the job references of candidates seriously in the running for the position. It's a waste of your time to check references that you won't use.

# SIFT THROUGH SOCIAL NETWORKS

So much has been said about social networking sites -- about their ability to reconnect people, to bridge geographical divides, to bring closer family and friends who have been separated for years. While this is well and good, social networking sites also play a pivotal role in helping us understand the machinations of someone's mind. This is particularly helpful when trying to go over the account of someone whom you are bound to have either a professional or a personal relationship with.

As a cautionary measure, though, make sure to avoid the pitfalls of cyber stalking. This happens when you become overly occupied with the details of somebody as posted on his/her account, a sort of fascination that hinges on the obsessive and disturbing. You do not want that to happen to you. What you want is to get an overview of somebody's personality without coming across as creepy. How do you do that exactly?

First thing is to identify the things you want to find out. If you are going over the account of someone who has invited you out for a date, you want to make sure that this person is not a sketchy character. You want to be assured that this person has a life, has healthy interests, has a circle of reliable friends, and not someone you would not want to have anything to do at all in real life. In other words, you do not want a detailed account of what this person has had for breakfast this morning; all you need is an assurance that this person is not someone you would not want to be associated with.

## Social Networks as Tools for Investigation

It would be worthwhile to point out at this juncture how social networking sites, such as Facebook, are increasingly being utilized by human resource personnel of different companies as efficient tools in assessing the hireability of certain applicants. In a study published February, 2012 in the Journal of Applied Social Psychology, it was found out that a person's Facebook profile reveals a more or less accurate portrait of how this person is going to perform at the job, should he or she be hired. The study took into account some of the things professional recruiters look into when trying to decide if they will hire an applicant or pass him/her over, such as intellectual curiosity, emotional stability, and relationship with others. Similarly, the study noted some of the "red flags" associated with people they would rather not pick. The study concluded that if someone is not likeable on Facebook, this person will more likely be less personable in real life.

Due diligence, however, must be exerted before passing judgment on a person on account of the little data that can be gleamed from their profiles. In fact, one of the aforementioned study's limitations is the fact that a single Facebook profile reveals only a little about a person, and that information derived from that page may not be entirely conclusive. Thus, to depend solely on Facebook for information would be unfair and a disservice to the person involved.

Regardless, it is easy to see why people would much rather go to Facebook to get a fairly accurate picture of who a person is and what his/her preferences or views are. In another study published in the Proceedings of the National Academy of Sciences (PNAS) journal early 2013, it was found that the sum of a person's public "likes" on things such as photos, videos, status updates, comments, and notes on Facebook may reveal a significant amount of information relating to a person's political views, sexual orientation, and other personality traits. This may not come across as an altogether surprising fact, but it nonetheless shows just how much data is available on social networks, and how such a massive volume of data paint an accurate portrait of who we are and what we believe in.

### Check other social networks, too

Facebook comes as a convenient starting point for doing background checks on a person, basically because it is the most popular social networking site at the moment. There are now more than a billion Facebook users across the world as of May 2013, according to latest figures from the mammoth site. From the looks of it, things are definitely going to be much bigger for the social networking behemoth. Despite this impressive number, however, there are a host of other social networks that attract their fair share of users. These are sites that you can also use to do a background check on somebody.

Micro-blogging site Twitter comes as a very convenient and user-friendly site that allows people to post status updates in 140 characters or less. The exponential growth of Twitter in the past couple of years was driven in large part by the ease with which the site operates and the enormity of data available. Part of its appeal can also be traced to its real-time news feed, which shows the status updates of the people you follow on the site.

What sets Twitter apart from Facebook is that it could be very personal and detailed despite the limitations set by the 140 characters. In fact, it is exactly this limitation in typing more words than needed that prompts users to be succinct and direct to the point, almost to the point of being enormously candid or even brutally honest. Similar to checking somebody's Facebook account, peering at somebody's Twitter account is bound to yield personal information relating to a person's character and preferences. The people that a person follows on Twitter are also reflective of the type of individual he/she is.

Photos are also a good way at identifying a person's character. Is he/she the artsy type? Does he/she have hobbies that show he/she is a regular person with real and actual interests? Are there photos of him/her with pets? Check if your date has a Flickr account and start from there.

But if you are looking for a person's professional background, you can head on over to LinkedIn to check his/her professional profile. LinkedIn is the networking site used by working professionals. It is particularly useful for human resource managers looking to fill up job vacancies, in much the same way that it is also useful for those wanting to verify a person's professional background.

At the end of the day, though, is it right to use somebody's Facebook and other social networking accounts as the complete basis of knowing who the person you would be dealing with is? The answer is of course, no. But it would be foolish not to tap existing information as a means of getting to know details about a person. After all, this is information available in public, which means the person deliberately put those pieces of information out for everybody else to see. The only thing to remember is to never go overboard. Know your limits of what you think are acceptable or not. This will help you in assessing which information you need, and which information are categorized as off-limits.

BONUS RESOURCE: If you are searching for someone on Facebook who has made their profile private, all is not necessarily lost. One clever way to still glean information about this person is to search google specific to facebook's site and it will bring up any additional pages etc. that the user has commented on. (i.e. site:facebook.com "John Doe")

# HOW TO PROCESS CULLED DATA

So you have done your research. Now what?

What you do with the information and knowledge you have acquired over the course of your research will prove to be very invaluable as you make your final decision. Given this data, will you allow the subject of your investigation to lease your property? Are you still going out with your subject for a date? Will you trust your subject to take care of your children while you are out of the house? Will you commit to a potentially expensive business venture with your subject?

There are varied ways to process the information you have acquired over the course of your research. One is to take them on face value. This is the easiest thing to do, but also the least introspective. It is easy to merely cast judgment on someone based on the things you may have seen, read, or heard from other people. However, this should not be your attitude. In fact, it would do well if you consider these things with a grain of salt until you have gathered sufficient evidence to prove that these things are indeed factual.

In this regard, learn to contextualize your data. For example, if you are a landlord looking for someone to occupy a property of yours, you want to make sure that your future tenant is financially capable of fulfilling his obligations. But what if over the course of your screening you find out that he has been evicted? The key is not to conclude right away as to the real score of such an eviction. After all, it is possible that such eviction may have been cause by anything other than the inability to pay. Identify the cause by calling the previous landlord, or asking the person himself/herself the details of what happened before. Learn to put things in perspective.

The same is true in the dating scene. Before you go out with somebody, you want to make sure that you are given the heads up as to who you will be meeting with. At the same time, you want to be assured that you are not going out with someone you do not want to have anything to do with. For example, married men with kids are definitely out of the question; they should not even be considered at all.

For babysitters, not only do you need to trust your gut instinct, you also need to put your kids' welfare as the top priority. You do not want to put that below anything else. If you have a difficult decision before you in choosing a babysitter, always err on the side of safety and security.

In the overall scheme of things, your background information on somebody can only do so much. After all, what information you have may be mere snippets of a person's real character and personality. You do not want to be overly reliant on bits and pieces of information. Try to assemble a holistic view of a person and take it from there. Remember to set everything in context for you to better understand the reasons and motives behind the things you were able to find out about a particular person.

BONUS RESOURCE: Don't have enough target information? These Websites Offer Free Background Checks!

- 
    http://freebackgroundcheck.freebackgroundcheck.org/3/Free_Backg round_Check.html
    - You can conduct a real do-it-yourself 100% free background check using this website. Their records are provided by the United States government and are free for the public to access. There are also paid options for more information.
    • http://www.beenverified.com/
    - The world's first and only free Background Check App. They have a mobile app version for iOS and Android.
    • http://www.dirtsearch.org/
    - One Stop Free Public Records & Background Checking. They have a mobile app version for iOS and Android.

# STRAIGHT FROM THE HORSE'S MOUTH

The previous chapters have provided you with details about how to conduct a basic investigation on a specific person that you are looking to have professional or personal relations with. This is well and good, given that it is natural among humans to be cautious and wary, especially when dealing with strangers for the first time. You want to have assurance that you are going in the right direction, and that you are dealing with a person you have absolute trust and faith in.

Essentially, whatever information you have managed to acquire should serve as a starting point for your eventual decision. For some people, this should be enough already. This is true, particularly when the information at hand speaks for itself and requires no further refuting. For example, how do you deal with someone who wants to lease a property of yours but is saddled by a really low credit score? Chances are you will skip this person's application in favor of someone who is on a more sound financial footing. For babysitters with a sketchy history, you might want to look past this person in favor of someone highly recommended by people you know.

However, it might also be best to consider conducting an interview with this person. Nothing proves or disproves your initial thoughts about a person more than a face to face conversation with that same individual. There are strategies to make this process as smooth and less problematic as possible. Here are a few:

1.    Do not be a hostile interviewer. Learn the benefits of subtlety. Do not be overly aggressive because that would only serve to make your conversation less fruitful and productive. Be friendly and accommodating. If you are interviewing a tenant, ask about his/her work, pets (if any),

people he/she thinks will be sleeping over to the property, his/her interests, and experiences with his previous apartment.

2.      Be direct when necessary. Even if you are keeping a friendly tone and demeanor, learn to ask the right questions. Be direct. If you are talking to a babysitter, ask about his/her experiences with kids and those kids' parents. Inquire if he/she is aware of first aid remedies and knows how to respond to emergency situations. Check if this person is adept at specific skills, especially when your kid is just an infant or one who requires special assistance.

3.      Be a good listener. Give the other side a chance to talk or explain some points. This way, both of you will be able to hear each other out and assess each other's personalities.

Screening people before meeting them is a natural mechanism for self-preservation. But know the limits of what it can do for you. Knowing everything about somebody before meeting him/her will prove to be a pointless exercise if you do not do your part to be trusted by the other party, too. Understand that the formation of trust in your relationship with others will spring only as a natural consequence of time and mutual faith in each other.

BONUS RESOURCE: Find additional tips online concerning how to conduct effective interviews for potential tenants and potential employees/partners by visiting our Additional Resources online, at: www.plaid-enterprises.com/bgc

# CONCLUSION

I sincerely hope the information contained within will help you begin securing background information on anyone you may be potentially entering into a personal or business relationship with. My intention is to offer you the tools needed to provide yourself with the peace of mind often lacking in these unknown ventures.

Having background information on someone is just the beginning. Once you have been assured that you are dealing with the right kind of people, make sure to foster a great relationship with them by being kind and sincere. After all, each relationship -- whether it is a professional or personal relationship -- should be rooted in trust and mutual respect for one another.

Finally, if you enjoyed this book, please take the time to share your thoughts and post a positive review on Amazon. I would greatly appreciate your support!

Thank you and good luck!

Benjamin Tideas

# ADDITIONAL RESOURCES

I'd like to invite you to visit my personal website for a list of additional resources and those found in this book - all in one convenient location! You can find it by following the links below:

BONUS RESOURCES to Perform Your Own Background Checks at
www.plaid-enterprises.com/bgc

Get my books for FREE! Visit www.plaid-enterprises.com